DECADES OF THE **20**th CENTURY

IN COLOR

THE 1920s

FROM PROHIBITION TO CHARLES LINDBERGH **REVISED EDITION**

STEPHEN FEINSTEIN

Library of Congress Cataloging-in-Publication Data

Feinstein, Stephen.
  The 1920s from Prohibition to Charles Lindbergh / Stephen Feinstein.— Rev. ed.
    p. cm. — (Decades of the 20th century in color)
  Includes index.
  ISBN 0-7660-2632-9
    1. United States—History—1919–1933—Juvenile literature.
2. United States—Social life and customs—1918–1945—
Juvenile literature. 3. Nineteen twenties—Juvenile literature.
I. Title. II. Series.
  E784.F45 2006
  973.91—dc22
                                    2005019863

Printed in the United States of America

10 9 8 7 6 5 4 3 2 1

To Our Readers: We have done our best to make sure all Internet addresses in this book were active and appropriate when we went to press. However, the author and the publisher have no control over and assume no liability for the material available on those Internet sites or on other Web sites they may link to. Any comments or suggestions can be sent by e-mail to comments@enslow.com or to the address on the back cover.

Illustration Credits: American Heritage Center, University of Wyoming, p. 41 (bottom); AP/Wide World Photos, pp. 53 (background), 55 (top, bottom), 56; Archive Photos, p. 40; Bert Randolph Sugar, *The Great Baseball Players from McGraw to Mantle* (Mineola, N.Y.: Dover Publications, Inc., 1997), pp. 31; Corel Corporation, pp. 8 (bottom), 15, 18 (bottom), 28 (background); Enslow Publishers, Inc., pp. 18 (top); Everett Collection, Inc., pp. 20, 23; Hemera Technologies, Inc., 1997–2000, p. 7; Huntington Library, p. 53 (inset); Library of Congress, pp. 6, 9, 10, 11, 12, 14, 17, 19, 24, 25, 26, 27, 28 (foreground), 30, 33, 36 (top, bottom), 37, 43 (top, bottom), 45, 47, 48 (top, bottom), 49, 50, 54, 57, 58; *Movie Star Postcards*, © 1986 by Dover Publications, Inc., p. 22; National Archives, pp. 4, 34, 38–39; Photo courtesy of the University of Illinois Archives, p. 32; Reproduced from the *Dictionary of American Portraits*, Published by Dover Publications, Inc., in 1967, pp. 8 (top), 35, 41 (top), 42; Stella Blum, ed., *Everyday Fashions of the Twenties* (New York: Dover Publications, Inc., 1981), pp. 16; The Stock Ticker Company <www.stockticker company.com>, p. 44.

All interior collages composed by Enslow Publishers, Inc. Images used are courtesy of the previously credited rights holders, above.

Cover Illustrations: AP/Wide World Photos; Bert Randolph Sugar, *The Great Baseball Players from McGraw to Mantle* (Mineola, N.Y.: Dover Publications, Inc., 1997); Corel Corporation; Library of Congress.

Every effort has been made to locate the copyright owners of the pictures used in this book. If due acknowledgment has not been made, we sincerely regret the omission.

 Enslow Publishers, Inc.
40 Industrial Road
Box 398
Berkeley Heights, NJ 07922
USA

http://www.enslow.com

Contents

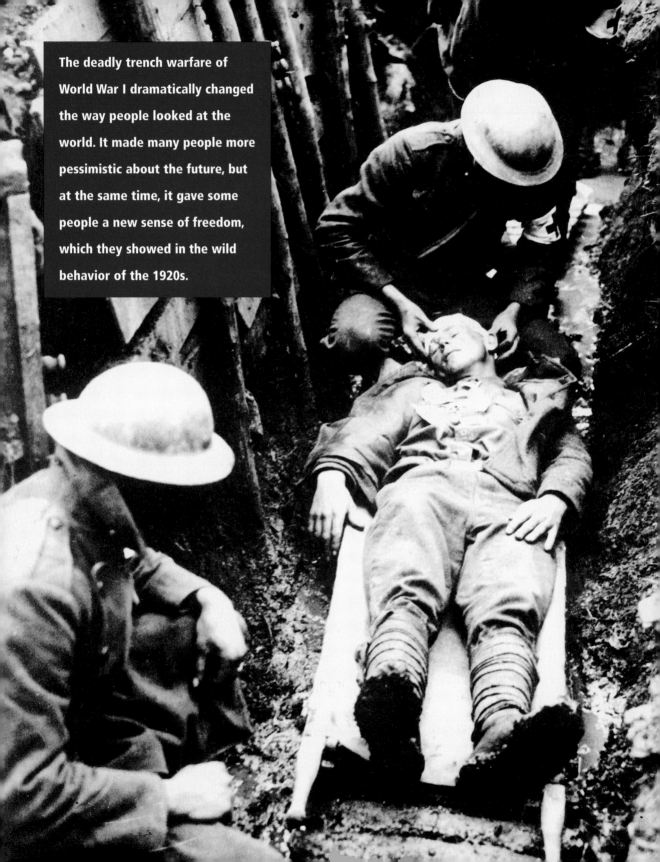

The deadly trench warfare of World War I dramatically changed the way people looked at the world. It made many people more pessimistic about the future, but at the same time, it gave some people a new sense of freedom, which they showed in the wild behavior of the 1920s.

For many Americans, the 1920s—often referred to as the Roaring Twenties—were a period of prosperity, with rapid growth in industry and new developments in the arts and entertainment. But the decade did not begin on an optimistic note. Although America and its allies had won World War I in 1918, the end of the war led to an economic slump.

The American economy began to recover and eventually prosper during the Republican administrations of Presidents Warren G. Harding and Calvin Coolidge. Both presidents encouraged the growth of big business. When Calvin Coolidge said, "the business of America is business," the nation took his words to heart.

Americans worked hard, but they also played hard. Not deterred by Prohibition—the ban on alcoholic beverages—many Americans went to speakeasies. There, they could drink illegal alcoholic drinks while dancing to the music of jazz bands. Women called flappers wore skirts with scandalously short hemlines. Having just won the right to vote, women felt freer to express themselves in new ways.

Meanwhile, many Americans invested in the stock market. But the stock market could not climb forever. A frenzy of speculation ended in the great stock market crash of 1929. The party was over.

Life Gets a Little Easier

During the 1920s, standards of living rose for most Americans, including the working poor, even though the majority of Americans worked long hours for very low wages. Basic utilities, such as natural gas, running water, and electricity became increasingly available in the home. Local governments provided water and sewage treatment and garbage collection. People lived healthier lives. With hot and cold running water, people bathed more frequently. By 1929, 71 percent of American homes had indoor bathrooms. With electric lights in the home, there was less danger of fire from kerosene lamps and gas lights. And thanks to gas stoves, the air inside the home was now free of coal dust and kerosene fumes. Middle- and upper-class families could afford to buy new electric appliances such as vacuum cleaners, washing machines, and refrigerators.

By bringing people within instant contact of one another, the telephone helped speed up the business world. Even President Calvin Coolidge (above) made good use of the phone.

Bringing People Closer

New forms of communication brought Americans closer to each other. The telephone, and then the radio, brought about major changes in the way Americans lived and worked. In 1915, coast-to-coast telephone service had begun. By 1921, 13 percent of Americans had telephones. A person on the West Coast was only a phone call away from someone on the East Coast. At the beginning of the decade, most Americans still wrote letters to stay in touch with distant relatives or friends. But as the years went by, more people had telephones in their homes. The telephone became essential in the business world.

The radio (below) was one of the most exciting new products of the 1920s.

On November 2, 1920, even as most Americans were yet to have a telephone conversation, another amazing device was introduced to the nation. On that day, radio station KDKA in Pittsburgh, Pennsylvania, broadcast the nation's first scheduled, public radio program. Only a small number of Americans got to hear the news broadcast that day on their brand new radio sets. But practically overnight, excitement about this new form of communication spread. By 1923, more than five hundred radio stations were broadcasting. Radio sales that year reached $60 million.

Listening to favorite radio shows became a popular family activity. As more Americans bought radios and tuned into broadcasts that featured music, sports, or news, American businesses began advertising on the radio. During the second

Henry Ford (below) revolutionized the automobile industry, but he did not "invent" the car. The automobile went through a long evolution even before Germans Gottlieb Daimler and Karl Benz invented the gasoline engine in 1885.

half of the decade, hundreds of radio stations were linked to form the two major radio networks, NBC and CBS. By the end of the decade, radios could be found in more than half the homes in America, and sales of radios had grown to over $842 million a year. In a single decade, radio had become a huge business and a major part of Americans' lives.

The Model T Ford

Americans love freedom. In fact, freedom is such a basic part of American culture that it is not at all surprising that Americans fell in love with the machine that gave them the ability to go wherever they wanted, whenever they wanted. Americans began buying cars as soon as they became available. In the 1920s, Henry Ford's Model T became the most popular automobile. Ford had lowered the price so that even the workers in his plants could afford to buy one. New Model Ts could be purchased for a few hundred dollars. A used Model T in good condition could be bought for as little as fifty dollars. There was such a high demand for the Model T that, in 1925, Ford's assembly lines claimed they completed a new Model T every ten seconds.

In 1927, Ford was facing increasing competition from General Motors' Chevrolet. To keep up, Ford introduced his Model A. The Model A was generally considered a vast improvement over the Model T. It quickly became the most popular car in America.

By 1927, the automobile had changed the lifestyle of millions of Americans. Many middle- and upper-class Americans moved to new suburbs, because the car gave them a convenient way to commute to jobs in the city. By 1929, there were more than 23 million cars on America's roads.

Getting There Faster

Passenger transportation took a great leap forward during the 1920s. Americans who needed to get from one city to another, or from coast to coast, could travel in luxury aboard plush trains. Throughout the decade, railroads were the preferred means of transportation. However, in 1927, another travel option became available. On May 20, Charles Lindbergh made the first successful solo transatlantic flight, from New York to Paris, aboard his little plane, the *Spirit of St. Louis*. The nonstop flight covered 3,610 miles and took 33 hours and 29 minutes. "Lucky Lindy" had made aviation history. He became an instant hero.

Less then three months after Lindbergh's epic flight, no fewer than eight airlines were offering regularly scheduled flights between various American cities. Earlier in the decade, airplanes had been used to deliver the mail. Now, airlines hoped to attract passengers, too. Although business was slow at first, the airlines could rightfully claim that they would get you there faster, although the trip would cost more. For example, in 1927, a trip from New York to Boston took five and a half hours by train and cost eight dollars. It took only three hours by plane, but cost thirty dollars. And one could travel

Upon landing in Paris, a smiling Charles Lindbergh (above) told the welcoming crowd: "Well, here we are. I am very happy." Lindbergh always said "we" in referring to his transatlantic trip, as he considered his plane, the *Spirit of St. Louis*, his partner in the endeavor. In fact, Lindbergh's book about the historic flight was entitled *We.*

from Chicago to San Francisco in 68 hours by train at a cost of eighty dollars, while it would take only twenty-two and a half hours by plane, but at a cost of two hundred dollars.

"Joe Sent Me"

The Eighteenth Amendment to the Constitution was ratified in January 1919. It banned the manufacture, transportation, and sale of alcoholic beverages. "Dry" organizations, such as the Women's Christian Temperance Union and the Anti-Saloon League, had succeeded in winning enough support to ensure passage of the amendment. As America entered the era of Prohibition, the new law seemed certain to put the thousands of bars around the country out of business. But apparently, it would have taken more than a new law on the books to change the lifestyles of millions of Americans.

The bars did indeed close down. But many of them soon reopened as speakeasies. Hidden away in rooms beneath or in the back of the former bars, the speakeasies served alcoholic drinks to customers who typically gained entry by giving secret passwords, often something such as "Joe sent me." The term *speakeasy* referred to the password ritual.

Some speakeasies were simple bars where people sat, drank, and talked. Others were elegant nightclubs where, in addition to drinking, customers were entertained by elaborate floor shows and danced to the music of lively jazz bands.

Considering that the main business of the speakeasies was against the law, how did they stay in business? After all, their locations were certainly known to the police. There is a simple answer to this question—bribery. Owners of speakeasies made regular payments to the police. Also bribing the police were gangsters known as bootleggers—powerful mob bosses, such as Al Capone and Bugs Moran—who sold the illegal liquor to the club owners. Of course, not all law officials were corrupt. Some businesses did close, if only temporarily, when the management and their customers were hauled off by the police after a surprise raid. But in general, Prohibition seemed to have created a win-win situation for the speakeasy owners, their customers, gangsters, and the police.

The situation caused a massive increase in corruption and the growth of organized crime. Powerful gangsters murdered anybody who got in their way. Machine guns and bulletproof getaway cars became essential elements of the gangster lifestyle. To many Americans, gangsters seemed to be heroic figures because of their defiance of authority. And the people who went to speakeasies believed that bootleggers were performing a useful service to society. But as gang violence grew worse, the romance faded. The final straw came on St. Valentine's Day in 1929, when seven men were massacred in a gangland killing ordered by Al Capone. Ultimately, Prohibition proved to have been a mistake. It would be repealed in 1933.

Alphonse "Al" Capone (above) was called Scarface because his left cheek had been slashed in a fight years before he rose to fame. Born in Brooklyn, he was the son of poor Italian immigrants. Despite the fact that he was well-known as a criminal, Capone was often treated like a celebrity as he rode around the city of Chicago in limousines.

Feminists and Flappers

Many American women in the 1920s, especially the younger generation, were eager to challenge society's traditional notions about the proper role for women. The women's suffrage movement, which had officially begun at the Seneca Falls Women's Rights Convention in 1848, ended with the ratification of the Nineteenth Amendment to the Constitution on August 18, 1920. Having won the right to vote, feminists now sought to bring about equality of the sexes. The League of Women Voters sought greater educational opportunities for women, and fought to eliminate laws that discriminated against women. The Women's Trade Union League (WTUL) fought to improve working conditions for women. And in 1921, Margaret Sanger founded the American Birth Control League (which would change its name to the Planned Parenthood Federation of America in 1942). The organization provided women with information about birth control.

Other feminists favored a more radical approach to women's rights. Alice Paul, the leader of the National Women's Party, led the fight for passage of an Equal Rights Amendment (ERA), which would guarantee equal rights under the Constitution. Many women, however, considered the ERA too extreme.

After women finally won the right to vote, they celebrated their victory, like suffrage leader Alice Paul, who toasted their success. Women also began to make other changes. In 1923, for example, Margaret Sanger opened the Birth Control Clinical Research Bureau in New York City, the first in what would ultimately become a nationwide network of hundreds of birth control clinics.

Many decades later, in the 1970s, feminists were still fighting for the ERA, but it was ultimately defeated.

While feminists sought to bring about change through political activism, other women brought about change in a different way. Young women who felt that they should be able to enjoy the same social and sexual freedoms as men came to be known as flappers. Such women hung out at speakeasies, danced, smoked cigarettes, drank bootleg liquor, and partied late into the night. More conservative members of society were shocked at the flappers' use of heavy makeup and outrageous dresses that revealed legs in silk stockings. Even worse, flappers kissed men in public and seemed to enjoy flaunting their irreverent behavior.

The Charleston

Many flappers went wild over a dance called the Charleston. The Charleston supposedly originated with African-American dancers in Charleston, South Carolina. It was characterized by fast-paced, jerky movements—a knock-kneed, heel-kicking, hip-swinging dance. While it tended to display the body because it required the dancers to wear loose clothing, the Charleston had a cheerful, saucy effect, rather than being seductive or sexy. People had so much fun dancing and just watching the Charleston, that a Charleston dance craze soon swept the nation. Before long, dancers were competing in Charleston contests. In 1924, a Charleston marathon at New York's Roseland Ballroom lasted for twenty-four hours.

Dance Marathons

During the 1920s, many Americans seemed determined to dance till they dropped. The main motivation was the cash prize awarded to the winning couple. Dance marathons took place throughout the decade all around the country. Young couples would dance for hour after hour—often day after day—struggling to keep moving. Often one or the other dance partner would fall asleep and the other would have to keep moving while supporting the sleeping partner. One by one, couples would collapse until one last couple staggered or crawled across the floor to collect the prize.

Among the more notable marathon dancers was Alma Cummings, who danced for a record-setting twenty-seven hours in New York in 1923. Her endurance seemed impressive, until June Curry danced for ninety hours in Cleveland that same year. Also in 1923, Homer Morehouse danced for eighty-seven hours. Unfortunately, Morehouse literally danced till he dropped—dead!

Short Skirts and Cloche Hats

Many women's fashions of the 1920s were inspired by the style of actress Clara Bow (below).

Flappers set the style for 1920s women who considered themselves free from traditional styles of dress. The typical flapper look was basically tubular—a little-boy look that de-emphasized a woman's natural curved form. The breasts were flattened, the waist was dropped to the hipline, and skirts kept creeping upward until they ended just below the knee. Flappers wore silk or rayon stockings with garter belts or rolled-over garters above the knee, and black patent-leather high-heeled shoes.

Because the flapper look required women to be thin, many women became obsessed with watching their weight. Tight corsets were replaced by looser, more comfortable undergarments.

Flappers wore their hair short, influenced by movie star Clara Bow. They hardly ever went anywhere without their bell-shaped, tight-fitting cloche hats (*cloche* means bell in French). In the evenings, however, flappers would often replace their hats with more exotic items, such as a jeweled comb or an ostrich-plume headdress. Formal evening wear often consisted of floor-length, backless evening dresses, often accompanied by long strings of beads.

In addition to hats, various other accessories such as scarves, handbags, jewelry, and cigarette cases were an important part of the flapper look. For a time, accessories decorated with ancient Egyptian motifs were the rage. In 1922, British archaeologist Howard Carter had excavated the tomb of King Tutankhamen in Egypt, discovering treasures that had been buried for more than three thousand years. When Carter toured America in 1923, a King Tut craze swept the country. Suddenly, Americans were fascinated with anything that looked Egyptian.

The tubular look was not limited to women in the 1920s. Young men's fashion also began to assume a tubular look. Men wore narrow-shouldered jackets that hung straight to the hips, and wide, loose-fitting pants. Around 1925, college men adopted Oxford bags, a more extreme style of wide-legged pants that originated at Oxford University in England. Oxford bags were so wide that the wearer appeared to be swimming in them. They typically measured about twenty-five inches around the knees and twenty-two inches around the cuffs. Also popular with

Fashion trends took their cue from the exotic Egyptian artifacts found in the recently discovered tomb of King Tutankhamen (below), better known as King Tut.

college men were the raccoon coat and the belted Burberry trench coat, another item influenced by British fashion.

Filling in the Blanks

In 1924, many Americans were spending their free time puzzling over clues to come up with the correct words to fill crossword puzzle grids. Crossword puzzles became a national craze, touched off by the publication of Richard Leo Simon and Max Lincoln Schuster's collection of crossword puzzles, *The Crossword Puzzle Book*. After the huge success of their first book, Simon and Schuster went on to build one of America's major publishing companies.

Before long, crossword puzzle contests were being held on college campuses. The University of Kentucky even offered a course in crossword puzzles. People could be seen working on crossword puzzles while dining in cafeterias, enjoying a picnic, or traveling on the train. Crossword puzzles must have been especially popular on the Baltimore and Ohio Railroad, because the railroad supplied dictionaries to passengers.

Exterior fashions (above) were not the only things to change during the 1920s. In 1923, Ida Cohen Rosenthal designed a brassiere that proved so popular that she and her husband founded the Maidenform Brassiere Company.

Twelve Amazing Words

While millions of Americans in 1924 were searching for the right words to fill in their crossword puzzles, many others believed that they had found a few special words that had the power to transform their lives. These people had come across

French psychotherapist Emile Coué's book about the power of mind over matter, *Self-Mastery Through Conscious Auto-Suggestion*. Coué's system was easy—all you had to do was repeat the same twelve-word sentence over and over again. For the next few years, Americans could be heard uttering the words, "Day by day in every way I am getting better and better."

Every decade seems to bring forth con artists who manage to make a lot of money from the wishful thinking of gullible people. In the 1920s, many Americans were convinced that, thanks to Emile Coué, the secret to good health and happiness was suddenly within their grasp. After all, Coué pointed to some miraculous cures that he attributed to his system. For example, one man had been cured of excessive yawning. And two boys who stuttered were now able to say without stuttering, "Good morning," and "I won't stutter anymore." Of course, Coué was never able to prove that his system had actually cured any serious problem. After a time, most Americans realized that if something sounds too good to be true, it is—and they swiftly abandoned Coué and his amazing twelve words.

Mah-Jongg

Millions of Americans in the 1920s suddenly found themselves uttering strange-sounding words such as *Pung* and *Chow*, and discussing Red Dragon, South Wind, and bamboo. They had become devoted fans of Mah-Jongg, an ancient Chinese game that was sweeping the United States. The game had complicated rules that were always

The crossword puzzle craze extended beyond the living room of the average American. Some talented people even solved crossword puzzles in unusual ways—like Harry Kahnel (below), who worked this giant puzzle upside down!

changing, and serious players studied rule books to keep up. The game was played with a set of 144 carved bone tiles, which were arranged on green-baize tables at elegant Mah-Jongg parties. Mah-Jongg sets were available in a wide range of prices. A fancy set could cost as much as $500, while a more humble set could be bought for just a few dollars. Many women stopped playing bridge and formed Mah-Jongg clubs instead.

The ancient Chinese game Mah-Jongg (above) was a big hit among Americans of the 1920s, who eagerly purchased Mah-Jongg sets in a wide array of styles.

Barnstormers and Flagpole Sitters

It seems that some people will do anything for money. A surprisingly large number of Americans during the 1920s participated in many kinds of wild and crazy stunts. Perhaps it was the general optimism of the times that led such people to believe that any stunt was worth trying. In the early 1920s, veteran pilots performed aerial stunts in rural America. They came to be called barnstormers. Sometimes, they would

Barnstorming—flying low over rural areas and performing dangerous tricks of aviation—became quite popular in the 1920s. Flying (right) was new, and most people still considered those who flew planes daredevils.

literally storm barns, swooping down to drop a chunk of ice on the roof in one typical routine. They would then land and bet the farmer that it would hail soon, even though the weather was clear and warm. They then took off and landed again, pointing out the ice to the farmer, taking the farmer's money, and laughing all the way to the bank.

Other popular aerial stunts involved wing-walking. The stunt person would climb out of his or her seat, usually in a two-seater plane, and walk out on the wing, performing various tricks while the plane's pilot carried out some tricky maneuvers. Although the wing-walker was protected by a leather and steel harness fastened to bracing wires, accidents often happened. Planes crashed, and wing-walkers and barnstormers were often killed. The aerial stunt business was dangerous. One barnstormer and wing-walker of the early 1920s who was not killed was pilot Charles Lindbergh.

Although flagpole sitters did not climb nearly as high into the air as the barnstormers, they remained above the ground for a much longer time. The flagpole-sitting fad began in Hollywood in 1924, when a theater hired Alvin "Shipwreck" Kelly to sit on the top of a flagpole fifty feet above the ground to draw crowds. For thirteen hours, Kelly sat on a small, rubber-padded seat strapped to the ball of the flagpole. He proved to be such a sensation that he was soon being hired by theaters and hotels all around the country. In 1927, in St. Louis, he sat on a flagpole for a record thirteen days! Flagpole sitting soon became a fad, and other people began sitting on flagpoles. In 1929, Kelly spent 145 days on flagpoles. That year in Baltimore, twenty people sat atop flagpoles during one week. Three of them were women.

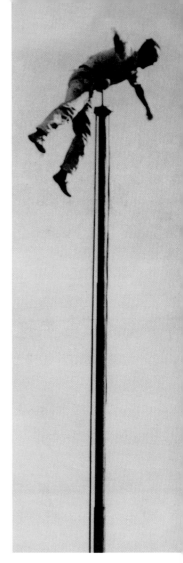

Fads that sweep the nation frequently make little sense, especially when we look back at them after a period of many years. Flagpole sitting is a perfect example. But people seemed to enjoy watching daring sitters, such as John Reynolds (above), perform their stunts.

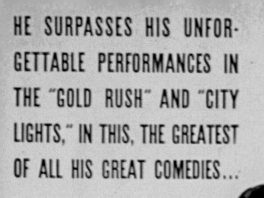

HE SURPASSES HIS UNFOR-
GETTABLE PERFORMANCES IN
THE "GOLD RUSH" AND "CITY
LIGHTS," IN THIS, THE GREATEST
OF ALL HIS GREAT COMEDIES...

Many actors were not eager to make the switch from silent films to the new "talkies." Charlie Chaplin (left) was among them. As time went by, however, most people in the film industry came to realize that sound was here to stay in the movies and decided to start talking.

Charlie Chaplin

IN

MODERN TIMES

Written, Directed and
Produced by
CHARLES CHAPLIN

Released thru
UNITED ARTISTS

"You Ain't Heard Nothin' Yet!"

"Wait a minute! Wait a minute! You ain't heard nothin' yet!" said Al Jolson in a movie called *The Jazz Singer*. Startled moviegoers in the audience on October 6, 1927, could not believe their ears. This was the first time they had ever heard a character in a film speak. Until then, all movies had been silent. The actors moved their lips and used exaggerated gestures to show what they were saying or feeling. The action on screen was frequently interrupted by printed captions. With the introduction of spoken dialogue, movies, called talkies, achieved a new degree of realism. Acting began to more closely resemble the way people acted in real life. Silent films had been popular with American movie audiences, but talkies led to a huge increase in ticket sales at box offices.

Not everyone welcomed the new talkies. Some actors who had built successful careers in silent film had trouble making the transition to talkies. Acting in sound films required different skills. In one case, silent movie star John Gilbert's career came to an end because movie fans could not reconcile Gilbert's romantic screen image with his high-pitched voice. Silent film comedians such as Charlie Chaplin, star of *The Gold Rush* (1925) and other comedy hits, were especially reluctant to add sound to their films. After all, the silent comedy had been a unique and popular form of art. Chaplin continued to resist the talkies, releasing his silent classic *City Lights* in 1931. But movie producers at the major Hollywood studios were aware that the future of film was the talkie. By the end of the 1920s, they had all but abandoned the silent film. Popular silent film comedians Stan Laurel and Oliver Hardy were just as popular once they began making talkies. Even Charlie Chaplin eventually began talking on screen in *Modern Times* (1936).

The Mouse That Launched an Empire

In 1923, Walt Disney and his brother Roy started the Disney Brothers Studio, Hollywood's first animated cartoon studio. One day while riding on a train, Walt began drawing a cute little mouse on his drawing pad. He called the mouse Mickey. On November 18, 1928, Walt Disney's *Steamboat Willie*, the world's first animated cartoon with synchronized sound, opened in New York. The cartoon featured Mickey Mouse and his girlfriend, Minnie. Sound was the key element in the movie's success. Mickey's fame quickly spread far and wide. In years to come, the Walt Disney entertainment empire—movie studios, TV network, and world-famous theme parks— would be built upon the popularity of the cute little mouse.

Jazz: From Speakeasy to Concert Hall

The Roaring Twenties were often called the Jazz Age, because jazz, with its strong beat and rhythmic syncopation, was the most popular music of the time. Jazz, the only art form invented in America, was African Americans' gift to the world. The earliest jazz originated in New Orleans. Its musical elements were derived from African-American brass marching bands and ragtime music from the saloons. Known as Dixieland, it was characterized by several musicians simultaneously playing their own improvisations based on the melody and chord pattern of the tune.

A colorized still (above) from the 1928 animated short *Steamboat Willie*, which introduced the famous Disney character Mickey Mouse.

By the middle of the decade, flappers and other patrons of the speakeasies were enjoying the lively jazz sounds of Louis "Satchmo" Armstrong and his Hot Five. The Hot Five consisted of Louis Armstrong on cornet (a type of trumpet), Kid Ory on trombone, Johnny St. Cyr on banjo, Johnny Dodds on clarinet, and Lil Hardin Armstrong (Louis Armstrong's wife) on piano.

Although many jazz fans consider Louis Armstrong the jazz world's greatest trumpet player, he was also a great singer. He had a unique, gravelly voice. Armstrong invented the jazz style of wordless singing known as scat. In it, the singer can imitate a horn solo or make use of other sounds or nonsense syllables. Other jazz singers, such as Ella Fitzgerald, would later become famous for their scat singing. What especially endeared Louis Armstrong to millions of fans around the world was his good-humored clowning.

Other important African-American musicians of the 1920s include the great blues singer Bessie Smith and jazz pianist-composers Duke Ellington, "Jelly Roll" Morton, and Fats Waller. Waller wrote more than four hundred songs and made around five hundred recordings during the thirty-nine years of his life. Among his most famous songs are "Honeysuckle Rose" and "Ain't Misbehavin'." Toward the end of the decade, a new type of danceable jazz that would become known as swing was becoming popular. Some people believe that the term *swing* originated with Duke Ellington's 1931 hit "It Don't Mean a Thing If It Ain't Got That Swing."

Many white musicians were influenced by the music of African Americans. White jazz musicians such as Benny Goodman and Bix Beiderbecke had a wide following. Bandleaders such as Paul Whiteman created smoother-sounding music that spread the appeal of jazz beyond speakeasies into the concert hall. Whiteman even hired classically trained composer George Gershwin to write a piece that wove elements of jazz rhythms and the feeling of the blues into a traditional concert piece. The world premiere of Gershwin's *Rhapsody in Blue* took place on February 12, 1924, in New York's Aeolian Concert Hall. Gershwin played the piano part, accompanied by Whiteman's Palais Royal Orchestra. *Rhapsody in Blue* became one of America's most popular concert pieces.

The Harlem Renaissance

The 1920s were a time of such great artistic achievement for African Americans that it is often referred to as the Harlem Renaissance. During this decade, New York City's Harlem became the cultural center for African Americans. All the top jazz and blues musicians of the 1920s played in Harlem's many nightspots. Entertainers such as Josephine Baker, Florence Mills, and Bill Robinson also performed there. In addition to the famous Cotton Club, the Apollo Theater, and the Savoy Ballroom, there were more than one hundred other places to listen to and dance to jazz.

The literary contributions of African Americans during this period were equally significant. Among the many fine writers

Blues singer Bessie Smith (above) was born in Chattanooga, Tennessee, in 1894. She joined a minstrel show on tour as a teenager before being discovered by a record producer. During her lifetime, her work was known mostly to her fellow African Americans, who bought millions of her records between 1923 and 1928.

One of the leading literary figures of the Harlem Renaissance, Langston Hughes (above) published all kinds of literature. However, it was his poetry and short pieces about a black man called "Simple" that won him most of his fame. Most of the "Simple" sketches had no plot. Rather, the character would give opinions about issues of the day in a plainspoken and emotional way. Hughes was proud of his African-American culture and used the Simple character to show how intelligent, yet uneducated, African Americans would behave in an integrated society if given the opportunity.

living and writing in Harlem at the time was poet Langston Hughes, who wrote his famous poem "The Negro Speaks of Rivers" at the age of eighteen. Hughes later took a musical approach to writing, often singing his "blues poems" aloud as he wrote them. Poet Countee Cullen eloquently expressed the despair of African Americans in poems such as "Any Human to Another." Claude McKay presented a realistic portrayal of black life in his novel *Home to Harlem* (1928). Other important writers included Jean Toomer, Arna Bontemps, and Zora Neale Hurston.

Weary As I Can Be

African-American artist Aaron Douglas produced this woodcut (above) for the October 1926 issue of *Opportunity*.

The Lost Generation

Gertrude Stein, an American writer living in Paris, was reportedly the first to refer to the other Americans in Paris in the 1920s as a "lost generation." Supposedly, World War I had so shattered the moral values of society, that many young Americans were now struggling to find meaning. And what better place to try to find oneself than in Paris?

The city of Paris, with its lively café society and atmosphere of cultural excitement, attracted American writers, artists, and composers. These and many others were drawn to Paris, seeking to escape a materialistic America, where alcoholic drinks were illegal and life was supposed to revolve around money and business.

Young American artists who were drawn to Paris, such as Man Ray and Alexander Calder, wanted to live and work in the

In 1921, Ernest Hemingway (above) went to Paris, where he became a well-known member of the "lost generation." Hemingway returned to the United States in 1927, where his writings won him great fame for many years to come.

same city as Pablo Picasso, Marc Chagall, and Joan Miró. New styles of art such as cubism and surrealism were being invented there every day. The geometrically patterned design styles on display at the Paris Art Deco exposition, which opened in 1925, would be a major influence on American architecture, interior design, furniture design, and fashion for years to come.

Young American composers such as Aaron Copland and Virgil Thomson wanted to study and write music in the same city as Igor Stravinsky, Darius Milhaud, and Eric Satie. And young American writers and poets made their homes in Paris because it was easier to get their works published there. Two American literary masterpieces of the 1920s were written in France: Ernest Hemingway's *The Sun Also Rises* (1926) and F. Scott Fitzgerald's *The Great Gatsby* (1925).

The Black Sox Scandal

Baseball was still the favorite spectator sport of millions of Americans in the 1920s, even though a major scandal had shocked baseball fans at the beginning of the decade. On September 28, 1920, eight members of the Chicago White Sox admitted that they had accepted $100,000 in bribes for intentionally losing the first, second, and final games of the 1919 World Series to the Cincinnati Reds. The eight men were immediately suspended and the team began to be referred to as the Chicago Black Sox. Baseball fans, however, soon got over their shock and focused instead on the sensational ball playing of a rising star of the baseball world.

The Home-Run King

George Herman "Babe" Ruth began playing for the New York Yankees on January 3, 1920. During his first year with the Yankees, Ruth batted .376, hitting 54 home runs, 9 triples, and 36 doubles. He scored 158 runs, batted in 137 runs, and stole 14 bases. The following year, 1921, he did even better, hitting 59 home runs, batting in 177 runs, with a total of 204 hits—including 44 doubles and 16 triples—for a batting average of .378. In 1923, Ruth hit 41 home runs and had a batting average of .393. That year, he was named Most Valuable Player in the American League. Also that year, the Yankees began playing in their brand new stadium in the Bronx, called Yankee Stadium. Ruth, to the delight of his fans, hit a home run on opening day. Ruth's superb playing attracted huge crowds. Fans began referring to the new stadium as "The House that Ruth Built." Throughout the rest of the decade, Ruth continued to amaze his fans, leading the American League in home runs from 1926 to 1931, hitting his record 60 home runs in 1927. After hitting his sixtieth home run, on September 30, Ruth exclaimed, "That's sixty home runs, count 'em. Sixty!"

The Yankees, with the help of the Home-Run King and another great batter named Lou Gehrig, won six pennants and three World Series championships during the 1920s.

"Shoeless" Joe Jackson (below) was barred from professional baseball after the Black Sox scandal. His disgrace introduced the saying, "Say it ain't so, Joe."

Touchdowns and Knockouts

Baseball was not the only sport to attract millions of fans in the 1920s. More and more Americans were drawn to football and boxing. Helping to boost the popularity of these and other sports were the nationwide radio broadcasts of sports events. Now fans around the country could share the blow-by-blow excitement of an event as it happened rather than waiting to read the scores the next day in the newspaper.

Harold "Red" Grange, known as the Galloping Ghost, helped make professional football a popular spectator sport. Grange achieved his greatest successes as a college football player at the University of Illinois, from 1923 to 1925. Fans were thrilled by his running and the apparent ease with which he scored touchdowns. During his three years at Illinois,

Yankee Stadium (above), which opened in 1923 in the Bronx, New York, was home to many great baseball players, including Lou Gehrig (right) and Home-Run King Babe Ruth (left). It is still known today as "The House that Ruth Built."

Grange played twenty varsity games, during which he ran a total of 3,637 yards and scored 31 touchdowns.

By the time he signed with the Chicago Bears in 1925, Grange had already attracted a huge following of fans. Thirty-six thousand of them paid to see him play his first game against the Chicago Cardinals on Thanksgiving Day, 1925. Although the game ended in a 0–0 tie, Grange, ever the crowd pleaser, had not disappointed his fans. At the close of the season, the Bears played against the New York Giants at the Polo Grounds in New York City. Seventy thousand spectators filled the stands, and countless others had to be turned away.

Boxing during the 1920s also grew into a popular spectator sport. Previously, boxing had been an unregulated sport, associated with criminal elements and gamblers. Because boxing was banned in many places, boxing matches were often held in saloons. After World War I, laws prohibiting boxing were largely done away with, and the sport came under the control of boxing commissions. Helping to popularize boxing were two of the greatest fighters of all time, heavyweight Jack Dempsey and lightweight Benny Leonard. Dempsey became heavyweight champion on July 4, 1919, when he took the title away from Jess Willard. Dempsey would remain champion for the next seven years, knocking out one challenger after another.

On September 23, 1926, Dempsey finally met his match. Dempsey and challenger Gene Tunney went a full ten rounds, and Tunney won by a unanimous decision of the judges.

The following year on September 22, Dempsey lost his second fight with Tunney. Unfortunately, he had stood over his fallen opponent as the referee counted for Tunney to get up, instead of immediately going to a neutral corner of the ring. Dempsey's mistake caused the referee to add four seconds to what should have been a ten-second count, allowing Tunney extra time to get up off the floor. Tunney then won the match, again by a unanimous decision, after the fight went the full ten rounds. Dempsey fans thought the decision was unfair. They would always blame the "long count" for their hero's defeat.

On July 21, 1921, Jack Dempsey (left) knocked out George Carpentier of France in the fourth round. On September 14, 1923, Dempsey knocked out Luis Angel Firpo of Argentina in the second round.

The League of Nations

World War I was supposed to have been "the war to end all wars." President Woodrow Wilson had told American soldiers that they were fighting "to make the world safe for democracy." Although later events would prove these goals to have been impossible dreams, Americans in 1920 could not have known that. When Wilson proposed a League of Nations (similar to today's United Nations) to help prevent future wars, few Americans were interested. Americans had little desire to be drawn into another conflict in Europe, should one arise.

The Treaty of Versailles between the Allies and Germany was signed in 1919. Germany was forced to accept full responsibility for having started the war and had to make huge war reparations. The treaty included the provision for a League of Nations. Although Wilson campaigned around the country for the treaty's passage, the Senate failed to ratify it, sensing the growing isolationist sentiment among American voters. When the League of Nations met for the first time in January 1920, representatives from forty-two nations were there. There was no American representative, however, nor did the United States ever join the league that Woodrow Wilson had helped create. Wilson's efforts to convince Americans of the importance of the League of Nations ruined his health. He was barely able to finish his term in office. Wilson died in 1924.

Outlawing War: The Kellogg-Briand Pact

Late in the decade, Americans overcame their fear of foreign entanglements. They enthusiastically supported passage of the Kellogg-Briand Pact, an agreement "renouncing war as an instrument of national policy." The pact was drawn up by French Foreign Minister Aristide Briand and United States Secretary of State Frank B. Kellogg. Although more than sixty nations endorsed the pact, it provided no measures for achieving peace beyond the moral force of world opinion. Unfortunately for the cause of world peace, the Kellogg-Briand Pact was a case of too little, too late.

The Reds Are Coming

A national hysteria known as the Great Red Scare swept through the United States in 1920.

The Kellogg-Briand Pact, the result of the efforts of Frank Kellogg (below), essentially tried to outlaw war in international politics. At the time, with the memory of World War I fresh in their minds, many nations hoped such a pact would prevent future conflicts. However, there was no way to enforce its provisions. Nations remained free to use warfare to solve problems, despite its "illegality."

Many Americans, frightened by the Bolshevik Revolution in Russia, became convinced that radicals were plotting to carry out a Communist revolution in America. Communism, which was based on the public ownership of property such as factories and land, included a goal of world domination. This caused Americans to fear that Communists would try to destroy their democratic system of government. Foreigners, especially recent immigrants, were looked on with suspicion. In 1920, Attorney General A. Mitchell Palmer rounded up more than four thousand people—alleged Communists, Socialists, and anarchists (people who want to get rid of all government)—and 556 of them were deported.

Also in 1920, Nicola Sacco and Bartolomeo Vanzetti, two Italian immigrants who openly expressed their anarchist views, were arrested for armed robbery and murder. In 1921, a jury found them guilty, and the judge sentenced them to die in the electric chair. Many Americans protested the verdict, believing that Sacco and Vanzetti had been condemned to death for their political beliefs. Demonstrations on their behalf took place in various cities around the country, and legal challenges led to a new hearing of the case, but the two anarchists were executed in 1927.

For a time in 1920, the United States was swept up in a wave of anticommunist hysteria, no doubt brought on by the success of the 1917 Bolshevik Revolution, led by Vladimir Lenin (above).

Led by A. Mitchell Palmer (right), the crackdown on Reds— Communists, Socialists, and anarchists— hurt the labor movement.

The Red Scare caused wide-spread fear when some people seemed to be jailed and even killed, like Sacco and Vanzetti (left), for political beliefs. Fears of foreigners and disputes over legal versus illegal immigration, especially from Mexico, helped inspire new immigration laws. Among these was the National Origins Act of 1924, which strictly limited the number of immigrants who could come to the United States, based on their country of origin.

Racism Rears Its Ugly Head

In 1921, 1924, and 1929, the federal government passed restrictive immigration laws, supposedly to prevent potential troublemakers from entering America. But there was an obvious racist element in the new immigrant quota system. The new quota system favored immigrants from northern and western Europe, especially Anglo-Saxons. It sharply limited the number of immigrants from southern and eastern Europe, especially Jews and Italians. Asian immigrants were almost totally banned, as were immigrants from Africa. But the new immigration quotas did not apply to immigrants from the western hemisphere. Indeed, during the 1920s there was increased immigration from places such as Canada, the West Indies, and especially Mexico.

Beginning in 1924, Mexicans crossing the border into the United States had to show proof of identity and other

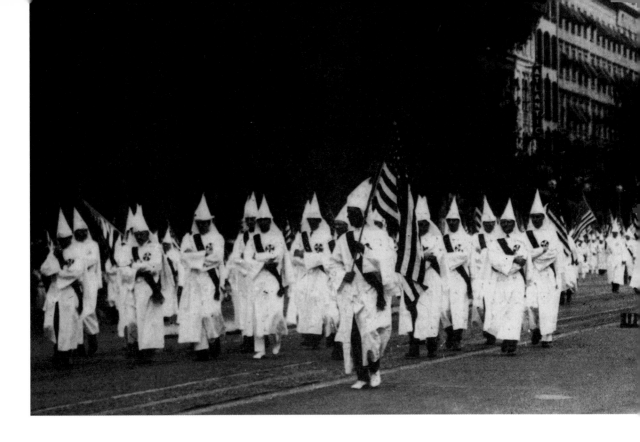

The Ku Klux Klan went through a revival in the distrustful atmosphere of the 1920s. Klan members even staged a huge march in Washington, D.C. (above). By 1929, however, the Ku Klux Klan had less than a hundred thousand members in the United States.

documentation. Many Mexican immigrants complied with this requirement. But many others ignored the law, avoided the border patrol, and entered the U.S. illegally. However, there was such a great need for cheap labor in the U.S., especially in the Southwest, that Mexicans were considered indispensable to the economy and were allowed to live and work there. Most Mexicans in the Southwest and California worked in agriculture or on the railroads. Others went to the Midwest and worked in steel mills, meat-packing plants, utility companies, construction, and trucking.

White racism in America during the 1920s reached levels not seen in many decades. Whites who hated African Americans, Jews, Catholics, and other ethnic and religious minorities joined the Ku Klux Klan, a white supremacist organization that enjoyed a surge in popularity during the 1920s.

The Klan, which began in the South after the Civil War, had been active in the years following the war. Its members intimidated and terrorized African Americans who had just emerged from slavery. Although Klan activity died down by the turn of the twentieth century, by the early 1920s, it had been reborn. It then spread into the Midwest, where it attracted a large following in places such as Indiana and Kansas. Its members burned crosses and engaged in other acts of intimidation and violence against blacks. Klansmen in the South lynched African Americans. (Lynching is the execution of a person accused of a crime without first holding a trial.) By 1924, more than 4 million Americans were members of the Klan. And in 1925, forty thousand Klansmen, dressed in their traditional white robes and hoods and carrying American flags, marched down Pennsylvania Avenue in Washington, D.C. Despite the apparent renewed popularity of the organization, membership declined during the second half of the 1920s.

Back to Africa

For most African Americans, the 1920s brought little relief from the poverty of previous decades. Those in the South lived in a strictly segregated society. Hoping to find better job opportunities, more than a million African Americans migrated from the mostly rural South to cities in the North. There, they faced discrimination in jobs as well as in housing, although they had far greater opportunities than in the South. For a time in the early 1920s, many African Americans became followers of Marcus Garvey, a Jamaican who had founded the Universal Negro Improvement Association in 1914.

Garvey wanted to instill a sense of racial pride in African Americans and create an independent black economy. As self-appointed "Provisional President of Africa," he planned to lead his followers in the creation of the Empire of Africa, a new African nation that would offer hope of a better life. But in 1923, before Garvey had managed to send a single African American back to Africa, he was convicted of mail fraud and sent to prison. Although Garvey was pardoned by President Calvin Coolidge after serving two years of his five-year sentence, his organization lost its influence.

Americans Vote for "Normalcy"

Republican presidential candidate Warren G. Harding won the 1920 election by a landslide

vote. Americans were in no mood for the Democrats' plans for involving the country in the League of Nations. They felt that Woodrow Wilson, a former college professor, had betrayed them by leading the nation into World War I. They liked Harding, who seemed to be a small-town, regular guy, just like the man next door.

Harding said he wanted nothing more than to bring the country back to "normalcy." To him, this meant an isolationist America in which the federal government would help promote the growth of big business. And Harding kept his promise. Unfortunately, he went too far out of his way to help his business friends. Harding's administration was notoriously corrupt. It became involved in one scandal after another, culminating in the infamous Teapot Dome scandal. In that episode, Harding's Secretary of the Interior, Albert Fall, accepted between $100,000 and $400,000 in bribes to lease government-controlled oil fields to his oil-business friends Harry F. Sinclair and Edward L. Doheney. The investigation of Teapot Dome was still going on in August 1923, when President Harding died in office.

Keeping Cool With Coolidge

Vice President Calvin Coolidge became president when Harding died. Coolidge was then elected president in 1924. The Republicans' campaign song, "Keep Cool and Keep Coolidge," was a hit with voters, who admired the candidate's cool, calm demeanor. Coolidge, known as Silent Cal, did not have very much to say, but apparently, this appealed to Americans at the time. By now, prosperity had returned to the American economy. Voters wanted a president who would continue the pro-business policies—such as tax cuts and protective tariffs—of Harding, but without the corruption. That is what they got.

Coolidge pretty much allowed business to take care of itself. And most Americans shared in the general prosperity.

Between 1923 and 1928, corporate income increased by 28 percent, average unemployment never rose above 3.7 percent, industrial workers' wages increased by 8 percent, and the average workweek was shortened to forty-five hours. Meanwhile, inside the White House, Coolidge would often sit in his office, feet up on the desk, and fall asleep. When his term was up, Coolidge announced his intention to retire to his Vermont farm. The "Coolidge Prosperity" almost guaranteed the election of another Republican president. And in 1928, Americans voted for Republican Herbert Hoover, who seemed to promise even greater prosperity for the nation.

Hoover and the Great Crash

In March 1929, business was booming, unemployment was low, and the future looked bright. A confident President Hoover told Americans that, before long, "poverty will be banished from this nation." A former mining engineer and self-made millionaire, Hoover seemed to be the perfect president to oversee America's growing prosperity. Hoover was a longtime friend of big business, having served as secretary of commerce in the administrations of Harding and Coolidge. In addition, Hoover had demonstrated compassion for the less fortunate, directing the Belgian Relief Commission and heading the United States Food Administration during World War I.

But things did not turn out the way Hoover had predicted. The stock market crashed in the fall of 1929, and the prosperity of the Roaring Twenties soon came to a screeching halt.

Despite his earlier efforts to help the poor during World War I, after the Great Depression began, many Americans would come to see President Hoover (top) as insensitive to the plight of the unemployed.

During the 1920s, the New York Stock Exchange (bottom) was a busy place that was often littered with tickertape at the end of a feverish day on the market.

The stock ticker was a form of telegraph machine that provided stock information to investors from coast to coast almost instantly. Old ticker tape was often used to shower parades that ran down New York City's Wall Street—a tradition often continued in parades today.

The booming economy of the 1920s had encouraged speculation in the stock market on a grand scale. Wealthy Americans were not the only ones to invest in the stock market. When it became clear how easy it was to make money in a rising market, many people who could not afford to gamble bought stocks anyway. Worse, they often bought stocks with borrowed money. The more money they made, the more they borrowed. By the summer of 1929, some people began to suspect that a crash was lurking just around the corner and began to sell their stocks.

A major sell-off of stocks did not occur until Thursday, October 24. On that day and the next, chaos and confusion ruled at the New York Stock Exchange. As stock prices fell, many investors had to come up with more cash or sell their stocks at a loss. Then on Tuesday, October 29, which became known as "Black Tuesday," the bottom fell out of the market. Countless investors lost all their money.

Within months of the crash, industrial production, prices, and wages declined, and unemployment rates began to rise. Hoover appealed to Americans not to lose confidence in the economy, but there was little he could do to prevent the economic collapse and the Great Depression that followed. Sadly, Herbert Hoover, who might have achieved great success in office had the good times continued, would go down in history as a relatively poor president.

The Rise of the Nazi Party

While most Americans in the 1920s tried to ignore what was happening in the rest of the world and enjoyed prosperous times at home, people in other countries were not so fortunate. European nations struggled to rebuild economies ruined by World War I. Although Germany successfully established the democratic Weimar Republic, the economy suffered under the burden of war payments demanded by the Allies. Unemployment was high, and inflation grew until German money was virtually worthless. Day by day, the value of the mark, Germany's currency, sank. A loaf of bread that cost less than a mark in 1918 cost more than 160 marks in 1922, and 200 billion marks in 1923! A wheelbarrow full of money was required to buy a single loaf of bread. Eventually, many Germans were unable to buy food.

On November 8, 1923, a right-wing political group known as the National Socialist German Workers' party (Nazis), led by Adolf Hitler, tried to overthrow the government in Munich. Hitler and his followers hated Communists, Socialists, and most of all, they hated Jews. The Nazis hoped that the German people, in their desperation, would support them. But the plot failed, and Hitler was thrown in jail. By the time he was set free, after nine months in jail, Hitler had written a book called *Mein Kampf* (My Struggle). In it, he set forth his plans for a powerful new Germany that he referred to as the Third Reich (empire). He also stated that the Germans were Aryans, a master race. All other races, such as Jews and Gypsies, were inferior, even subhuman, in his eyes.

The massive war payments forced upon Germany by the Treaty of Versailles led to high unemployment and soaring inflation. This caused such misery among the German people that they became eager to follow any leader who could promise them better lives. Despite his radical views, Adolf Hitler (below) was just such a leader.

Hitler's hateful message did not fall on deaf ears. The Nazi party slowly but surely grew.

Events in 1928 would prove especially bad for the future of Europe and the world. That year, Hitler's Nazi party won a dozen seats out of 491 in Germany's Reichstag (legislature). Perhaps this did not seem very important at the time, but it was a major step in Hitler's climb to power and to eventual Nazi control of Germany.

Dictators in the Soviet Union and Italy

Meanwhile, Russia and Italy were already under the iron rule of brutal dictators. By 1920, the Communists in Russia had won the civil war that followed the Bolshevik Revolution of 1917. In 1922, the country was named the Union of Soviet Socialist Republics (USSR), or Soviet Union. When Vladimir Lenin, the "Father of the Revolution," died in 1924, a political power struggle began between two of his key followers—Leon Trotsky and Joseph Stalin. In 1928, Stalin, the ruthless "Man of Steel," solidified his control of the Communist party and began transforming the Soviet Union into a totalitarian regime in which the central government would control every aspect of people's lives. By 1929, Stalin was the undisputed leader of the Soviet Union, and Trotsky was forced into exile.

By 1928, Benito Mussolini had gained total power as *Il Duce* (the leader), the dictator of Italy. Mussolini's rise to power began early in the decade. He and his followers, known as Blackshirts, carried out a campaign of terror against Communists and Socialists. In 1922, Mussolini had led fifty thousand Fascists in a march on Rome, where he demanded that King Victor Emmanuel III put him in charge of the government. Once in power, Mussolini began to get rid of

Italy's democratic system. He banned labor unions and political parties that opposed his own, and he imposed strict government censorship on the media. He became popular with many Italians because he got things done. So while their democracy was disappearing before their eyes, many did not object. After all, working conditions improved, the economy grew stronger, and best of all—the trains ran on time.

The Chinese Civil War

At the end of the 1920s, America and Europe were not the only places facing difficult futures. China had been in conflict throughout the decade. Those who sought to unify the country under a strong central government faced almost impossible odds. Warlords in various provinces of the huge country fought among themselves for power and influence. In an effort to gain the upper hand over the warlords, Communists formed an alliance with the Nationalist Kuomintang, which was led by Jiang Jieshi (or Chiang Kai-shek). The alliance did not last long. In April 1927, Jiang's forces carried out a massacre of Communists in Shanghai, and the two groups became bitter enemies. Shortly after Jiang became president of the Nationalist Republic of China in 1928, the Communists and Nationalists began fighting a bloody civil war that would last for many years.

Eventually, the Communist forces would win the Chinese Civil War (below), forcing Jiang's troops to flee to the island of Formosa, now called Taiwan. On Taiwan, Jiang (above) set up a democratic government, which continued to claim to be the legitimate government of China. Meanwhile, Mao Zedong established a Communist government in mainland China, which came to be called Red China.

The Fight for Indian Independence

Trouble of a different sort was brewing in another part of Asia during the 1920s. India at that time was a part of the British Empire, but demands for independence were spreading. Leading the growing independence movement was Mohandas K. Gandhi, whom Indians referred to as the *Mahatma* (Great Soul). Gandhi preached nonviolence as the most effective way

Mohandas Gandhi, known as the Mahatma, is seen left, at right, with his fellow Indian leader Jawaharlal Nehru. Gandhi, who urged a return to the simple lives the Indian people had led before British colonialism had begun to industrialize the nation, fought for many years to win India's independence.

to achieve independence. He called his approach *satyagraha* ("truth force," or passive resistance). Gandhi urged Indians to engage in nonviolent civil disobedience to protest unjust British laws. He encouraged Indians to boycott British cloth and weave their own instead. Gandhi practiced what he preached. He refused to pay British taxes or vote in elections. He led strikes and protest demonstrations and engaged in hunger strikes. He was often jailed for his actions. Unfortunately, some Indians did not always refrain from violence, and some protests led to bloody riots. Gandhi's nonviolent struggle would continue for several decades, and the goal of an independent India would finally be achieved in the late 1940s.

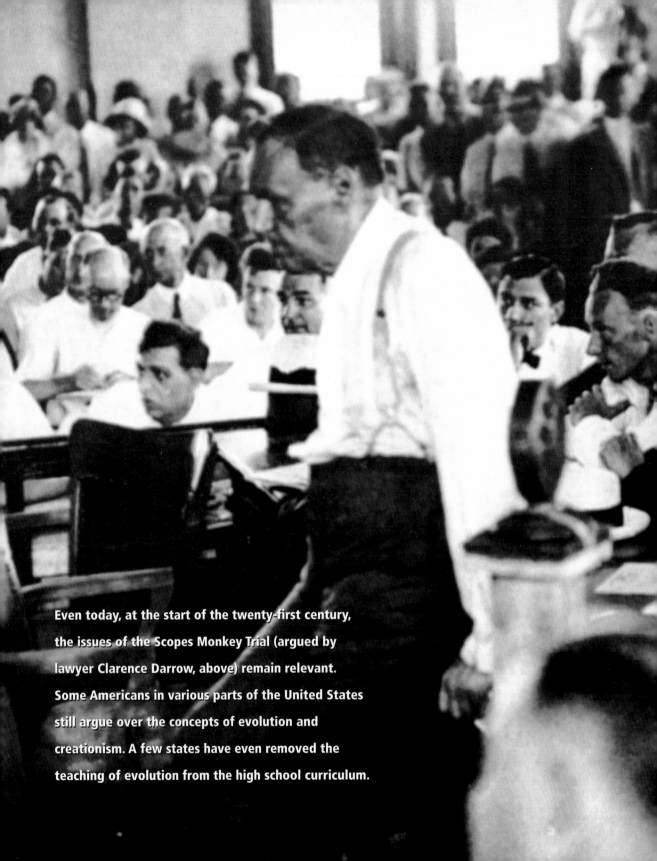

Even today, at the start of the twenty-first century, the issues of the Scopes Monkey Trial (argued by lawyer Clarence Darrow, above) remain relevant. Some Americans in various parts of the United States still argue over the concepts of evolution and creationism. A few states have even removed the teaching of evolution from the high school curriculum.

Science on Trial

On April 24, 1925, John T. Scopes, a high school science teacher in Dayton, Tennessee, gave a classroom lecture on Charles Darwin's theory of evolution. For this, he was promptly arrested. In March 1925, the state of Tennessee, catering to the wishes of Fundamentalist Christians, had passed a law forbidding the teaching of evolution in public schools. Fundamentalists, who believe in a literal interpretation of the Bible, regard Darwin's theory about human descent from a lower order of primate as heresy (against the teachings of Christianity).

The American Civil Liberties Union (ACLU) hired famed attorney Clarence Darrow to defend Scopes. The state's prosecutors hired William Jennings Bryan, a former presidential candidate and secretary of state. During the two-week so-called Monkey Trial, which began on July 10, 1925, Darrow poked numerous holes in the case of Bryan, who presented himself as a "biblical expert." Bryan's answers to Darrow's questions about the Bible often sounded ridiculous and caused laughter in the courtroom. Although Scopes was found guilty and sentenced to pay a fine of $100, Darrow had succeeded in arousing the public's interest in Darwin's theory of evolution because the trial had received so much attention in the press. Eventually, Darwin's theory became a standard part of most school science programs. Sadly, Bryan died of a heart attack five days after the trial.

An Expanding Universe

As recently as the 1920s, people believed that the Milky Way galaxy, in which Earth, the other planets, the sun, and all the stars are located, was the entire universe, and that the universe had always existed in a constant, relatively stable, form. But in 1924, American astronomer Edwin Hubble made a startling announcement. The previous year, he had learned that the fuzzy points of light, or nebulae, he had been observing through a 100-inch reflecting telescope at Mount Wilson in California were actually clusters of stars. And he concluded that these clusters of stars were individual galaxies. Indeed, the Milky Way was just one among many galaxies, and Hubble had figured out the distance to nine of the nearest ones.

Then Hubble made another incredible discovery. In 1929, he announced that the universe is expanding, with the galaxies

Sun

rushing away from each other. The farther away a galaxy is from us, the faster it is moving. This ratio is now known as the Hubble constant. Hubble's discovery later led scientists to theorize that the universe had begun in a "big bang," and that it has been expanding ever since. Today, we know that there are at least 100 billion galaxies that can be seen by telescope, and each galaxy contains about 100 billion stars. Thanks to Hubble, we can see how truly vast the universe is.

"Seeing As Well As Hearing by Radio"

In the 1920s, Americans were still excited about their amazing new radios. But work was progressing on the development of an even more amazing device. In 1923, David Sarnoff,

who would become president of RCA (Radio Corporation of America) in 1930, made the following prediction: "I believe that television, which is the technical name for seeing as well as hearing by radio, will come to pass in the future." That year, a Russian immigrant by the name of Vladimir Zworykin invented the first television camera. He called it the iconoscope and applied for a patent. In 1924, Zworykin patented the kinescope, a television picture tube using a cathode-ray tube (CRT). The following year, he applied for a patent for color television, which was granted in 1928.

The television (above), first introduced to a limited community of scientists in the 1920s, would become more widely available after making its debut at the World's Fair in 1939.

Television was first introduced to the public in 1928, although on a very limited scale. That year, the Daven Corporation of Newark, New Jersey, offered for sale the first commercial television receiver for $75. Also that year, television station WZXAD in Schenectady, New York, offered the first scheduled television service, broadcasting the news and the first televised play, J. Hartley Manners's *The Queen's Messenger.* Although television would not become widely available until the 1940s, Sarnoff's prediction proved to be remarkably accurate.

A view of the interior of the Holland Tunnel shortly after it opened for traffic in November 1927 (top) and a modern-day view of the tunnel's New Jersey-side entrance (bottom).

Cars Under the Water

On November 13, 1927, people in New York and New Jersey were able to drive their cars under the Hudson River—without getting wet! On that day, the world's first underwater automobile tunnel opened for traffic. The Holland Tunnel, named after Clifford Milburn Holland, chief engineer of the tunnel, connected Manhattan to New Jersey. A system of fans and suction ducts were built into the tunnel's twin tubes in order to ventilate the interior of the tunnel.

Saving Lives With an Iron Box and Two Vacuum Cleaners

Iron lungs (below) helped many polio patients breathe. The devices enclosed the entire body except the head.

In 1928, Philip Drinker and Louis Agassiz Shaw created a machine that could help people breathe. At the time, many people, including soon-to-be-president Franklin D. Roosevelt, suffered from polio (poliomyelitis), a disease of the central nervous system that caused paralysis. Often, the lungs were affected, and it became difficult or impossible to breathe. Drinker and Shaw's machine, called an "iron lung," helped people breathe. The first iron lung was built with an iron box and two vacuum cleaners. The patient would lie in the iron box chamber and the vacuum pump pushed air inside, causing the lungs to inflate. Many lives were saved by the iron lung, which saved people from suffocating.

An Accidental Discovery

One day in September 1928, Alexander Fleming, a Scottish bacteriologist, was about to throw away a culture plate he had prepared several weeks earlier with the common infectious bacterium known as *Staphylococcus aureus*, when something caught his eye. When he took a closer look, he noticed that there were spots of mold growing near the edge of the plate, and that the bacteria near the mold had been killed. For many years, Fleming had worked to discover a substance that would destroy disease-causing bacteria. Suddenly, by chance, he seemed to have found what he was searching for. He identified the mold as *Penicillium notatum*, a mold found on Camembert cheese. He called the bacteria-fighting substance in the mold *penicillin*. Unfortunately, at the time, Fleming was not able to find a practical method of extracting it from the mold. It would be many years later, in the 1940s, that Fleming and his colleagues Howard Walker Florey and Ernst Boris Chain would find a way to purify penicillin. The discovery would eventually save millions of lives.

After Alexander Fleming (above) made his breakthrough discovery, the path was paved for pharmaceutical companies to learn how to mass-produce penicillin.

Two young flappers dance the Charleston just outside the Capitol Building in Washington, D.C., in the late 1920s. The Roaring Twenties are still fondly remembered for their newfound social freedom and the wild behavior, especially among women, who had so recently won the right to vote and begun to take their place on the American political scene.

An Amazing Decade

The 1920s were a relatively prosperous period for most Americans. It was a time in which America retreated in isolation from the troubles of the world. A series of conservative Republican administrations in Washington catered to the interests of big business, and many corporations grew powerful and prosperous. The American experiment with Prohibition led to the widespread popularity of the speakeasy, which in turn provided a setting for the exciting new sounds of jazz and a place for flappers and others to kick up their heels to the dance craze known as the Charleston. Unfortunately, the speakeasy also provided a way for gangsters to grow rich selling bootleg whiskey, and this led to the rise of organized crime and mob violence. Many Americans tried to get rich another way by speculating in a rising stock market, and found, to their sorrow, that nothing goes up forever. The great stock market crash of 1929 seemed to guarantee that the next decade would not be at all like the Roaring Twenties.

Timeline

1920   In January, the League of Nations holds its first meeting; On January 3, **Babe Ruth** is traded to the New York Yankees; On August 18, the Nineteenth Amendment to the Constitution is ratified, giving women the right to vote in the United States; On September 28, eight members of the Chicago White Sox admit accepting bribes and playing to lose in the 1919 World Series; In November, radio station KDKA broadcasts the first scheduled radio program; Republican **Warren G. Harding** wins election to the presidency on a platform urging a return to "normalcy"; Great Red Scare begins; **Sacco** and **Vanzetti** are arrested.

1921   **Margaret Sanger** founds the American Birth Control League.

1922   British archaeologist **Howard Carter** discovers King Tut's tomb in Egypt; Russia is renamed the Union of Soviet Socialist Republics, or Soviet Union; **Benito Mussolini** leads a march on Rome, demanding that he be put in charge of the government.

1923   More than five hundred public radio stations are broadcasting; Archaeologist **Howard Carter** visits the United States on a lecture tour, setting off a "King Tut" fad; **Babe Ruth** is named Most Valuable Player in the American League; Yankee Stadium opens in the Bronx, New York; **Marcus Garvey**, leader of the "Back to Africa" separatist movement, is convicted of mail fraud and sent to prison; In August, **President Harding** dies in office; **Vice President Calvin Coolidge** becomes president; In November, the Nazi party tries unsuccessfully to overthrow the German government; **Vladimir Zworykin** invents the first television camera, called the iconoscope.

1924   In February, **George Gershwin**'s *Rhapsody in Blue* premieres in New York City; At the height of the Charleston craze, a Charleston marathon at New York's Roseland ballroom lasts for twenty-four hours; **Richard Leo Simon** and **Max Lincoln Schuster** publish *The Crossword Puzzle Book*, which starts a crossword puzzle craze; Psychotherapist **Emile Coué**'s book *Self-Mastery Through Conscious Auto-Suggestion* wins many followers; **Alvin Kelly** starts the flagpole-sitting craze; **Woodrow Wilson** dies; In November, **Coolidge** is elected president; **Vladimir Lenin**, leader of the Soviet Union, dies; **Edwin Hubble** announces that the Milky Way is just one of many galaxies; **Vladimir Zworykin** invents the kinescope.

1925 Charlie Chaplin's *The Gold Rush* is released; **F. Scott Fitzgerald**'s *The Great Gatsby* is published; **Harold "Red" Grange** signs with the Chicago Bears, attracting a huge following and helping make professional football a popular spectator sport in the United States; Forty thousand members of the Ku Klux Klan march in a parade through Washington, D.C.; For two weeks, starting on July 25, the Scopes Monkey Trial takes place.

1926 **Ernest Hemingway**'s *The Sun Also Rises* is published; On September 23, heavyweight boxing champion **Jack Dempsey** loses to **Gene Tunney**.

1927 Ford introduces the Model A, an improvement on the Model T; In April, **Jiang Jieshi**'s Nationalist forces attack Communist forces at Shanghai, permanently separating the two groups; On May 20, **Charles Lindbergh** makes the first solo nonstop transatlantic flight, from New York to Paris, France; On September 30, **Babe Ruth** hits his then-record sixtieth home run for the season; On October 6, the first spoken-word film, *The Jazz Singer,* opens in theaters; **Sacco** and **Vanzetti** are executed.

1928 **Claude McKay** publishes *Home to Harlem*; In August, several nations sign the Kellogg-Briand Pact, which will attempt to outlaw war as a means of solving international problems; In September, **Alexander Fleming** accidentally happens upon the mold that will eventually lead to the development of antibiotics; In November, Republican **Herbert Hoover** wins election to the presidency; Nazi party candidates win a dozen seats in the German legislature; **Joseph Stalin** takes control of the Soviet Communist party; **Jiang Jieshi** becomes president of the Nationalist Republic of China; The Chinese Civil War begins; **Vladimir Zworykin** receives a patent for his color television; The Daven Corporation offers the first commercial television for sale.

1929 **Joseph Stalin** becomes the dictator of the Soviet Union; There are more than 23 million cars in America; **Edwin Hubble** announces that the universe is expanding; On February 14, the St. Valentine's Massacre (ordered by **Al Capone**) takes place in Chicago; In March, **President Hoover** predicts a coming end to poverty; During the summer, some people begin to sell their stocks; On October 24, a large sell-off of stocks occurs; On October 29, the stock market crashes, setting off the Great Depression.

Further Reading

Books

Evans, Harold. *The American Century*. New York: Alfred A. Knopf, 1998.

Gow, Mary. *The Stock Market Crash of 1929: Dawn of the Great Depression*. Berkeley Heights, N.J.: Enslow Publishers, Inc., 2003.

Jennings, Peter, and Todd Brewster. *The Century*. New York: Doubleday, 1998.

Kent, Zachary. *Charles Lindbergh and the Spirit of St. Louis in American History*. Berkeley Heights, N.J.: Enslow Publishers, Inc., 2001.

Wukovitz, John F. *The 1920s*. San Diego, Calif.: Greenhaven Press, 2000.

Internet Addresses

The Coolidge Era and the Consumer Economy, 1921–1929
http://lcweb2.loc.gov/ammem/coolhtml/coolhome.html

Jazz Age Culture
http://faculty.pittstate.edu/~knichols/jazzage.html

Tennessee vs. John Scopes: The "Monkey Trial"
http:// www.law.umkc.edu/faculty/projects/ftrials/scopes/scopes.htm

Calvin Coolidge
http://www.whitehouse.gov/history/presidents/cc30.html

Index